WARRIORS & WILD DAISIES

Warriors & Wild Daisies

LEE MAYWOOD

NATIVE
EDEN
BOOKS

Content

This is dedicated to Molly, my beautiful mother
who gave me lifelong poetry

~ In loving memory

Like the ancient flow of tides turning, new seasons stirring
the moon waning, so are the changing seasons of life
connecting women in friendship, strength and wisdom
as beautiful and perennial as the flowers growing wild in
the meadows. On and on through women's hands and hearts
we share our stories, our joys, our heartbreaks, our victories
our experiences, our love. We support and uplift each other
as our sisters have done for countless years before.

~ 1 ~

She wore her scars
like a string of pearls
showing how beautiful
they had made her

Women

Unfold me into shades
of sunshine and passion
clay and wildflowers
let moonlight seep through
the curves and folds
of the body I can call my temple
of the mind I call my own
I stand on the shoulders of brave, fierce, unstoppable women
our sisters in history who stood their ground
who stood up for liberation, culture, free speech,
equal opportunities, voting rights, women's rights
and did not give up the fight
We stand on the shoulders of fierce, brave unstoppable women
passion, resilience and grace passed down the line
by grandmothers, mothers, aunties, sisters
walking before us, paving our way
uniting and fighting for women to have their say
sharing resilience, courage and strength
together we stand
united we rise
spreading our arms
spreading our hearts
the women of earth rise

Firewood Banksia
(Banksia Menziesii)
Fowering Autumn & Winter

~ 3 ~

She comes and goes like summer rain
drenching life with rainbows and puddles

~ 4 ~

Sometimes you just want to
punch Cupid in the face
turn those pouty, cute, rosy lips
into big, red, messed-up melons
and tell the smug little Roman love god
where he can shove his arrow next

~ 5 ~

The world smiles
when you
dance
the rhythm
of your own
heart

Jervis Bay

Softly I walk among the ancient trees
whispering and swaying in the summer breeze
lost in the allure and the shadows cast
the tranquil peace in a forest vast

A hint of sea salt beckons me nearer
ushers me forward on impulsive feet
shows me a place where the forest grows clearer
where land and ocean horizons meet

Sunlight dances on aqua blue reaches
scurrying foam laps on white sandy beaches
and the birdsong, echoes like water and laughter
filtering down from the green forest canopy

The arc of the bay with its chiseled rocks strewn
like the towering echoes of ancient stone ruins
the beautiful bay, a great oval mirror
reflects the sun's rays in a dancing white shimmer
and she speaks in a way that I dare understand
of all the treasures we hold in the palm of our hand
nature's artwork painted and carved into the land

Wildflowers

Pick wildflowers from the wilderness of your heart
weave them into a wreath for your hair
Yellow puffs of wattle from childhood
The teenage girl passing by
deep red Waratahs reaching for the sky
The busy mother finding grounding
among the orange Banksia flowers
blooming out her window
The old woman gathering wildflowers
to set on her kitchen table
Everlasting daisies, yellow and cream
in the wise woman's hands

All the wild blooms, the perfumes
the thorns, the breeze, the sunshine
the vast, wild seasons
which sculptured and coaxed these flowers to bloom
Pick wildflowers from the wilderness of your heart
weave them into a wreath for your hair
to honor the child, the girl, the woman, the mother
All the wild blooms of life's seasons
that made you a wise, beautiful, incredible woman

Old friend

Old friend, come, sit a while
it is all out on the table between us, I reach for your hand
let my heart fall out on my sleeve
despite the miles and the hard years
between us is something beautiful.
I let go of everything
smile at your gypsy heart
it belongs to the wide blue sky.
Always did.

How to have a spontaneous garden tea party

1. Bake a chocolate cake or other suitable favorite

2. Go into your garden, find a shady tree or spot among flowers. Set out chairs and a table. Pick flowers, arrange them in your hair.

3) Go inside, put on a summer dress. Call your five favorite women, friends, sisters, daughters etc invite them over for a spontaneous tea party.

4) Boil a pot of tea, set your outdoor table with fancy teacups, fresh flowers and chocolate cake. (Champagne or wine can be substituted for tea if needed. Guitars, shakers, hand drums, are also an option.)

5) Spend hours chatting, laughing, singing and relaxing with your women in the garden.

~ 10 ~

Yeah, I just made all those mistakes with my own raw talent

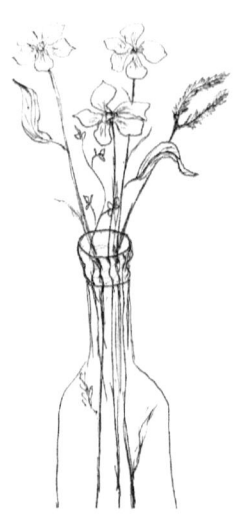

~ 11 ~

Take time
to do something beautiful
everyday

~ 12 ~

Mother's rose

Her inner beauty and serenity, never for a moment waned
as the light faded pale on her gentle face
and the ebb of life drew to a close
I knew her love would infuse our hearts
forever
like a deep red rose
as I held her hand
and quietly prayed
while she drew her final breath
for a mother's love shines endlessly bright
never dimmed by the shadow of death

~ 13 ~

True love
is tangled
in the everyday
moments
we share

Women drumming

Last night we went to the forest
women, sisters, warriors
we brought our drums
we brought our hearts cracked open
we brought our fears and heartaches and scars
worn as pearls around our necks
to show how beautiful they made us

The moon was full, raw
calling out to our wild woman
'Dance barefoot, drum loud
get messy, get real, get dangerous
We let it all wash away
like ocean droplets
running down the curves of our skin

And we drummed
loud and heartbroken
and we drummed, fierce and magnificent
we danced bare, untamed, unapologetic
among those old trees
Following the animal trails
weaving through the forest

we danced down to the beach
empty
silver in the moonlight
danced into that fierce, dark ocean
hearts naked, eyes clear, wings unfolded
Sirens, mermaids, oracles, lionesses, Elders
earth mothers, Aunties, medicine women
wise old hags, Amazons, warriors, she-wolves
The rest is secret women's business

~ 15 ~

Sorry, I didn't hear the phone. I was way too busy singing really loudly in my kitchen, pretending I was a rockstar while I washed the dishes

Australian Boab
(Adansonia gregorii)

~ 16 ~

There are women who always have stylish outfits and perfect hair. And there are women with wild hair and practical clothes who often have sand or dirt between their toes. They are my sort of women, the wild-hair ones.

How to make a wish on shooting stars

1. Wait till night.

2. Grab a picnic blanket and find a keen friend. (Bringing a picnic of wine and cheese is also optional.)

3. Find a soft, spongy patch of grass, position picnic blanket dead center. Lie down together looking into the night sky. Feel awestruck.

4. As you wait, pretend you know a lot more about stars and constellations than you really do, start pointing out random clusters of stars and give them names.

5. When a shooting star appears, resist the urge to squeal as you have been pretending to be something of a star expert up until now, don't blow your cover. Stay calm. Take a deep breath. Close your eyes and make a wish, ensure your friend is also making a wish.

6. Wait for wishes to come true.

~ 18 ~

My jungle garden

I love my jungle garden, with all her life, vibrant colors and wisdom. Knowing exactly when to flower, when to rest and be still. Following the seasons, gathering the birds and insects and wildlife in the deep green arms of a forest hug. Always reaching for the sky, always reaching for the stars, that wild, leafy canopy.

Spend time in gardens. Listen to the quiet wisdom among the moss and trees, the sunlight dappled branches swaying in the breeze. Feel the slow rhythms, the buzz of bees, the soft flowers, the peaceful hum of life nurtures your heart.

March 4 justice

No longer
will we be reduced
by your gender violence
by your unpunished crimes
against women
We are the victims
of the allegations you dismiss
We are angry, we are seething
as you attempt to diminish our voices
hush us with threats
political, discriminatory, economical, personal

No longer
will we fold up our wings
to crush into the confines
of your unjust acceptance
as you huddle behind professional, political circles
turning blind eyes for your mates

No longer will we hush the wild drumming of our hearts
that pound for justice
to end discrimination, violence, rape

We call for justice
We call for change
We call for recognition
from decades of crimes, corruption, injustice
Authority wielded as a weapon
of mass destruction
on a gender
to slice away consequence
responsibility
guilt
While you degrade us
beat us down
destroy our rights
with the flick of a pen
then wash your hands clean white
together
professionally, politically
and try not choke on a latte of
watered-down sexual assault consent laws.
On a morning when you are all too busy
to listen or care.
No longer
will we be reduced
by your gender violence
by your unpunished crimes
against women

~ 20 ~

Each day
she showed me
her little imperfections
I loved her more

Eucalyptus / Gum tree
(Eucalypteae)

The old blue sky

After all is said and done
and fought for
differences put aside
are we not all dancing, under the same blue sky?
To our heart's own beat
the music of our soul
swaying and tapping feet
to Mother Earth's slow rhythms
her vast heartbeat
the gentle seasons turn
as we dance our lives, under this old blue sky

~ 22 ~

Well yes, if I had kept my mouth shut
there would have been peace, but I also
would have had to crumple up my soul.
Screw that.

~ 23 ~

Always try to be a first-rate, graceful woman
by kicking-booty, being powerful and embracing your true
worth

Xanthorrhoea Australis

Traditional wisdom

Xanthorrhorea Australis

Ancient and slow growing with a lifespan of over 600 years, this iconic Australian naive plant flowers after bushfires, helping native birds and wildlife recover by producing a nutritious food source. With flower stalks towering up to 4 meters tall it produces hundreds of flowers and seeds along the stalks that can be used to harvest highly nutritional food and nectar. The leaf bases are also edible, containing about 5% sugar, yielding a sweet nutty flavor. Xanthorrhorea Australis have long traditional uses spanning thousands of years for medicinal remedies, food, perfumery, personal care, making products and in spiritual practices. The pulp inside the top of the plant is consumed for upset stomach. The resin is used as an incense, perfumery and in soap making. The resin from the trunk has been used as adhesive for building and creating many products. A sweet, highly nutritional beverage is made from the nectar of the flowers. Meditating under or near an ancient plant in flower is said to increase mental and spiritual clarity and enlightenment. The crushed seeds make nutrient rich flour, and can be added to many dishes. The flower spikes can be used to create fire when rubbed with hard wood.

~ 24 ~

When you
broke my heart
you rearranged
my mind
and liberated
my soul
to shine

Sure, I can be bad tempered, inflammatory, outspoken
and annoying. I'm also kind when it matters and loyal
I wont just be your friend in the fair weather
In the storms, I'll roll up my sleeves, wade through the mud
dig trenches and brave the deluge to be at your side
We are county women, that's what we do
We are tough, innovative, supportive and no nonsense
When it matters, we make it count

This taking the high road business seriously impedes my creative plans.

Medicine women's traditional wisdom

Australian Boabs (Adansonia Gregorii) can hold over 100,000 liters (26,000 gal) of water in their trunks. Medicinal uses: The bark and leaves have medicinal qualities for supporting healthy function of various body systems, including; digestive, cardiovascular, liver, hormonal, blood sugar regulation, bone density, liver, vision and respiratory. They can treat fever, chest infections, and help stress reduction. Traditionally also used for spiritual enlightenment, grief & emotional stability. High in vitamin C, calcium & other nutrients

Afternoon among the vines

It is a lazy Sunday afternoon
winding down in a little winery
out the back of a country road
the grey skies looking down on me
Old stone walls and worn wood
remind me of our farm in my hometown
the dust and the years
have claimed her now
but she makes me smile all the same
Makes me remember
my childhood dreams, my name

Got a past at my side
that should have been left behind
and a heart waiting at my doorstep
My heart is on my sleeve
and miles are in my mind
I have carved up some roads
to leave them behind.
Distant mountains stretch away
in shades of blue
and the trees are busy turning
their autumn hue

The hired singer smiles
as he watches a child wander by
and strums his guitar
like he has caressed it all his life
It's a well-worn old thing
seen better days
but the sound coming out
feels like a summer haze
so mellow and gold
and strums at my soul
like something else

His eyes wander the crowd
then out to the distance
like the lyrics
crack open his heart
to the world for a moment
The words float away
lazy as the summer breeze
His voice melts me
has the quality of an old Kombi van
bouncing down a dusty road
waves rolling to the west
surfboards in the back
windows all down, searching
for the waves that are best
Yeah, this stranger is singing to my soul
cracks me open for a while
Honestly, I could stay

~ 28 ~

Sometimes the greatest action
is to stop and simply be still

Kangaroo Paw
(Anigozanthos)
Australian Native

Colors

I have screamed my pain
at your tear-stained face
beat your heart till it is black and blue
I have lost myself
in your deep embrace
loved and lived far more deep and true
for the colors your soul
paints in this world
for the black and white
you tear apart

~ 30 ~

When I grow up I'm going to be a pirate

~ 31 ~

Inside every brave heart
is the long, hard road
it took to get there

Xanthorrhoea Australis

~ 32 ~

In the waves

They talked till the cafe kicked them out at closing time. Wandering aimlessly along the footpath, the tune of an old record playing 'Summertime' floated out an open window. She twirled to the music. He put his arms around her as they swayed to the old jazz under the dim glow of street lamps, the misty rain curling her hair into ringlets and covering them both in tiny silver droplets. She grabbed his hand, pulling him through the streets. The evening air felt raw more than cold, fog hanging low over the parking area by the beach. The pale sliver of a dying moon hanging overhead. She kicked off her shoes, ran along the sand, arms outstretched, looking up at the moon. She stopped, stood still, gazing at the waves. Reaching up her hand, her movements graceful and impossibly beautiful in the moonlight, she gathered her mane of dark locks over one shoulder. Unclasping the buttons of her summer dress at the nape of her neck, shivering slightly, the dress slipped off, lay in soft folds of deep green in the sand around her feet. She picked it up, threw it onto the rocks. He couldn't move with her there, silhouetted by the silver moonlight reflecting against the ocean. She waved her hands, smiling, beckoning him to join her, then dashed off into the waves. But he just stood there as she laughed and hooted, lied about the water not being too cold and called him chicken for not running straight in. What she didn't realize was it wasn't the cold water. It was the way the moonlight shone on her body and how her hair tumbled down her back. It was the side of her face and the way she ran her fingers through the water that had him transfixed on the shore. When he managed to pull his shirt off and splash in after her, she said nothing, just took his hand. Lacing her fingers through his, they floated in the moonlight swirling around on the currents. Floating on their backs, gazing into the stars, that quiet infinite moment lay against him forever. In that moment he loved her. In the following years, he loved her more. Every spontaneous dance on the beach. Campfires, cooking marshmallows and telling stupid jokes. Hikes together and road trips. Rainy Sunday mornings, twirling his fingers through her hair while she lay in his arms chewing on the end of her pen, asking him random questions to fill in the crossword, he loved her more.

Manuka Tea Tree / Manuka Myrtle
(Leptospermum scoparium)

~ 33 ~

Reality continues to crumble my stupendous plans

~ 34 ~

Does Wonder Woman have to iron her cape
or does she always just wash it on permanent press
and pretend the crinkles and wrinkles don't exist?
Like I always do to avoid ironing

For equality, for pride

If I reached out
I could probably touch your heart
So why not?
The sun is on my fingertips
If I reached out
I could probably see your point of view
So why not? The choice is in our hands

Feel the vibration of many feet marching
for equality.
For pride.
For our lands.
For freedom.
Find the rhythms
that liberate your soul
and dance them
Uninhibited.
Unashamed.
Find languages that are universal
and speak them
find love that is universal
and spread it

If I reached out
I could treat you as my kin
So why not? Acceptance is in reach
and the space between our hearts
in truth is minimal
So why not? Why not?

Feel the sunshine on your skin
feel the rhythm of the earth through your feet
clear your mind and shine from within
Stand up strong for what you believe
Stand up tall for the way you see it
Keep wide open for people's different views
their cultures, their dreams, their feelings, their truths

Look into the nearer now
look into the clearer now
see details and intricacies overlooked
the dreams and gifts right in front of us
treasured moments, we forget are beautiful
in the rush of the mundane.
Look into the clearer now
keep your eyes and heart wide open

Feel the liberation
of many feet marching
for equality. For pride.
Finding voices
long silenced
Dust rising
sun shining
bodies moving
minds moving

Change, rising
Feel the music of change and sovereignty with your soul
Feel the rhythm of equality in your heart
as we dance our lives, under this old blue sky

After all is said and done and fought for
differences put aside
Are we not all dancing, under the same blue sky?
Under the *same* blue sky
To our hearts own beat
the music in our soul
authenticity in our feet
earth's slow rhythms
her vast heartbeat
the gentle seasons turn
Dancing the universal languages
it is an ancient thing
it is a tribal thing
it is a heart thing
the way it moves us

Feel the liberation of many feet marching
for equality
for pride.
All voices matter
All cultures matter
All histories matter
All voices matter

~ 36 ~

The years in
your arms
have made
my life
so beautiful

Whenever I'm about to do something stupid and risky, I think, is this a good idea? The answer is often no. Then I end up doing it anyway, somehow.

Echinacea, Coneflower
(Echinacea Purpurea & Angustifolia)

~ 38 ~

Place your hand on my beating heart
while you fly away with the angels
I promise to still see silver linings
and still reach for those distant stars

~ 39 ~

Let's linger the hours away
rambling barefoot, hand in hand
on abandoned beaches
watching clouds tell their stories
discussing love and music and art
silhouetted by the tides
the joyous, wild gratitude of birdsong
filling our souls
and forget about
everything else

Medicine women's traditional wisdom

Lemon Myrtle
(Backhousia Citriodora)
Australian Native
Use leaves all year round
Medicinal: Antimicrobial
Anti-viral
Anti-inflammatory
Antioxident
Powerful Whole body tonic

~ 40 ~

Ocean song
Sinking into the earth
it is a slow grace
found with many roads traveled
fears and loves faced
Give it time
breathe the air in deep
these things of the earth
we get to keep
Beckoning softly
these deep blue skies
remind our wings
they are free and wise
and been folded far too long
The waves flow in, the ocean's song
draws us to the endless swell and beat
of our hearts and lives and creativity
Seen your soul before
somewhere down the line
it is faded, but clear
Sisters, brothers, we have shared some time
joining hearts and hands
walking our way
through these old sacred lands
Sinking into the earth with love and grace
sinking deep in her embrace

give it time
breathe the air in deep
These things of the earth
we get to keep

~ 41 ~

No, sorry, I can't work this weekend. I will be way too busy having leisurely brunches and wandering hand in hand through the art galleries, the park, the antique shops with my love, maybe playing our favorite music really loud, and slow dancing in our living room, then curling up together by the wood fire listening to the rain on the tin roof

~ 42 ~

She turned heads
because she
was wildly
unapologetically
just herself

Australian Boab
(Adansonia gregorii)

~ 43 ~

Life gives you lemons and sugar, you know what to do girl

Mountain Pepperbush
(Tasmannia Lanceolata)
Uses: Spice & medicinal
strong antimicrobial
antioxidant, treats scurvy
high in vitamins,
increases energy & staminer
Leaves, all year round,
berries & flowers in summer

– A poem about miscarriage and endometriosis (trigger warning)

Not for shooting stars

My body abandons herself
wages war on her own flesh
I crumble under the weight of that knowledge
knowing so well what it means.
My courage, clutched like a rope around my throat
as I face each curve of this path
the constant red drip of my own blood leaking out
doesn't just make my body ache,
it devastates my heart.

How I would love to know what it was like to stay a mama
hold my own child to my breast
watch her grow and thrive and love her with all my heart
But tears can't wash away what is real.
I have cradled this torn uterus
through too many years of blood
agony
miscarriage.
Cradled my growing babes with pure love
to a death, far too soon

brought about by my own endometriosis ridden body
Wished on each not-for-shooting star
till my baby fell from my sky
I have lost my mind to patch up my womb
watched her lasered
and burnt
and cut
and stitched
in the hopes she could carry a child full-term.
'Just have children, that often fixes it.'
'Yep, thanks Doc, I'll give that my best shot.'
I cradle my belly, with a uterus that is all torn up again
and the gift, the hope, that miracle, my baby
that dream slips through my fingers again.

I ache as I let go of the dreams
a shattered goodbye to the brave little soul
who I never had a chance to hold.
Not even for a single moment.
I let go of hope
and instead make a plan.
So what does it mean to be strong?
I just ache inside and out.
It is simple.
It is basic
it's just accepting what is
and from that place of reality
I need to find my feet
still let my soul shine

Because beyond the dirty, cracked glass
that is currently the window to my soul
outside, there is still a beautiful world.

~ 45 ~

In journeys of the heart
you can only take
what you can carry

~ 46 ~

She fell, like autumn leaves
softly, gracefully, quietly

Little girl

Trailing shadows
dawn emerging
slowly softly
orange creeping into pink
lifting away the night sky
The low crackle of crickets
and marsh frogs
the only sounds
in that vast dewy expanse
of ryegrass
ghost gums
bloodwoods
The rest of the world lies sleeping
except a little girl
a blue ribbon in her tangled hair
hands holding a brown teddy bear
her bare feet dangling
off the edge of that old wooden veranda
feathery ryegrass tips
tickling her soles
mother nature's artwork
a landscape painted with sunrise gold and silver dew
tickling the little girl's young soul

~ 48 ~

Love is
when her smile
makes your day
beautiful

~ 49 ~

What, do you expect me to do all this housework? Fat chance, when the sun is shining, the weather is perfect and the ocean is calling.

Together

Take my hand
and untame your heart
I'll take your hand
while you walk through the dark
the soft glow of moonlight
walking under the stars
searching for answers
that are missing

~ 51 ~

Umbrella

We run through the dark streets
under our umbrella, in the lamplight and rain
and somewhere lost in time
your fingerprints
trace down my spine
and the lines
on your palm
point my way
We are riding through the streets like careless lovers
laughing, dreaming

~ 52 ~

I'm only irreverent, obscene and opinionated
when it is necessary, granted, it is often necessary

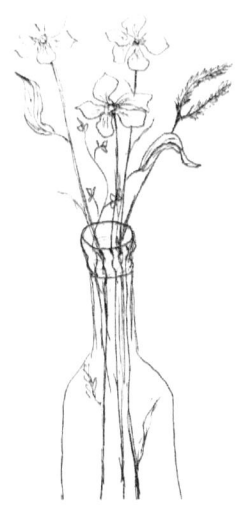

~ 53 ~

How to hula hoop like when you were a kid

1. Notice someone has brought a hula hoop to the gathering

2. From afar, watch other adults have a crack at it and fail miserably

3. Begin to suspect you can do a lot better, after all, you were quite the hula hooping champion as a kid

4. Stride over and announce loudly you are going to give it a go

5. Flex your arms and legs a couple of times to build suspense. Grasp the hula hoop, expertly place it around your waist

6. Twirl and shimmy those hips, baby, count how many times the hoop rotates around your waist. (Please note, a slight rotation as hoop slithers down your body and falls to the ground does not count as one)

7. Wait for cheers and applause. Raise your hands above your head triumphantly

~ 54 ~

In an argument the only word
that actually matters is sorry

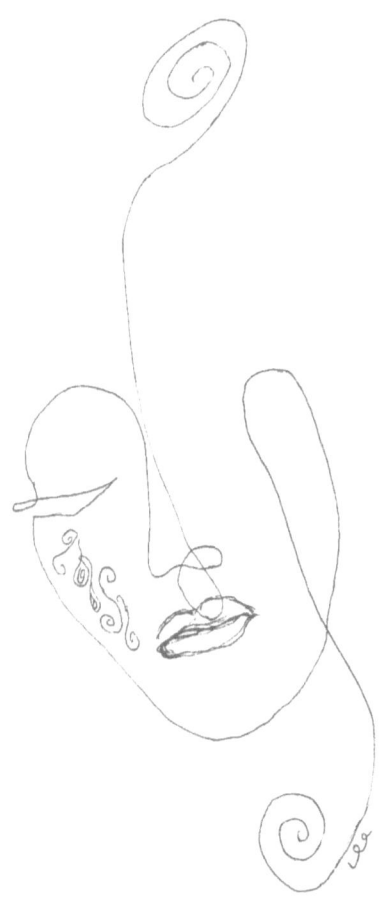

~ 55 ~

Certain opinionated barefoot irreverence is welcome

~ 56 ~

Sorry I cant get to the phone at the moment
I'm too busy frolicking in the ocean pretending I'm a mermaid

Crumpled linen

Winter just washes away, while I am searching for why
I speak the words, but my head is far away in the sky
and I know that you'll use me
however you want to.
Can you tell I have been down for a while?
And I feel like I am losing some ground to my soul
he is no longer inside me
you can take that however you want to
and I'm shedding the place that I thought I belonged to

I am washed down like bourbon, then slammed on the table
I'd stop if I could, run if I was able
Where would I run?
Maybe winter will just wash this away

Life is running through my soul
like sand through an hourglass
I avoid your eyes
because my heart is in my mouth
and my soul is naked and screaming out loud
and my silence you can't take
you can take that however you want to

you shake your head, avert your gaze, walk on by

I feel like I am losing control of my ground
he wanders inside and yells so loud
I am glued to the place where I thought I was found
my hands on the door, trembling
yeah, I'd go if I could
my heart is on the ground
his hands are steel blades on me
I'm washed down like bourbon
then slammed on the table

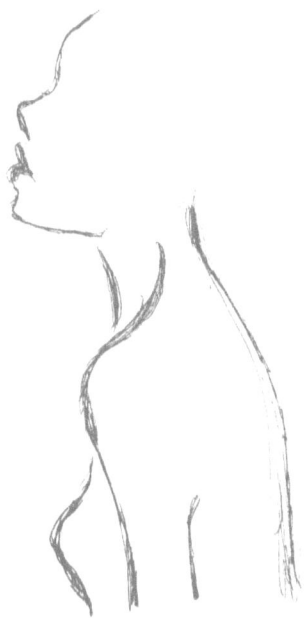

~ 58 ~

Like artists we painted
our life
full of colors
now my tears
are like rainbows
running down
my cheeks

~ 59 ~

A yarn about being a solo woman in business, banks and property buying

When I was about thirty I was going through marriage separation. We met young. I was nineteen, married a few years later and we spent a decade or so as best friends, lovers and partners in crime. But eventually the marriage had fallen apart and I'll take a good chunk of the blame for that. So there I was divorced. My friends were planning weddings, having babies and building dream houses with their husbands and I was on my own, broke, feeling sort of liberated, sort of terrified, pretty much a failure and entirely determined. My endometriosis was giving me hell, stage 4, severe hemorrhaging and crippling pain 24/7 with no cure or relief in sight. I felt beaten, heartbroken from years of multiple miscarriages, faded dreams and a lost love. So just to stress myself out a bit more I moved interstate and decided I would try opening my own business. I figured it was a really good time to make a new business work with the excellent motivation that if I didn't make it succeed I wouldn't be able to afford to eat. I created and printed out poorly designed brochures and read books on business. When the endometriosis pain would let me, I roamed the streets with my A4 sized business brochures in a bag slung over my shoulder. I asked local retailers if I could leave a brochure for the staff to read. I took some of their business cards and began promoting their businesses along with my own. Figured I may as well seeing as I was walking around everywhere doing my own promotions anyway, why not create some extra business for other local shops too. I was very grateful when some shop owners kindly offered to stick my brochures up in their shopfront windows for exposure to passing traffic. I was super shy and introverted. God, I always felt so nervous, overwhelmed and nauseous walking the streets promoting myself and my new business. However, I stuck with it, determined. Unless the endometriosis pain had me bedridden, I handed out brochures every day, besides Mondays. Mondays I went to the beach. Yeah, it was all old-school 'feet on the pavement' back then, no online advertisements. I am showing my age. I also created 20% off discount vouchers and rambled the streets giving them to people. I ventured into markets, fairs, tourist hot-spots and other busy places handing out these vouchers. I can tell you, my introverted little heart was just dying inside, with my stomach knotting every step of the way. I loathed promoting. Funnily enough, people who I handed discount vouchers to in the street started saying things like:

'Oh my God. This is fate. I saw your brochure the other day in a shop and now *here* you are in *person* giving me a discount voucher so randomly. It must be fate that I should use your business.'

Of course it wasn't exactly random fate. I had spent thousands of hours putting up my brochures locally in every willing shopfront window, at every industrial site, on every public noticeboard, into hospitals, commercial buildings, schools, universities, daycare centers, manufacturing and mechanical workshops, petrol stations, sales yards, stuck them on random fences, telegraph poles, at sporting grounds, canteens, children's parks. Anyone who had functioning eyes had seen one of my brochures. It wasn't exactly random coincidence and fate, it was tactical hard work that resulted in those people receiving a discount voucher after seeing a brochure. But if they wanted to call it fate, great, who was I to tell them any different, they could believe it was fate if they wanted. From all the promotion I did get thousands of wonderful, loyal long-term customers and my business grew and thrived and yes, I could afford to eat.

I started to dream about owning a little cottage of my own. A place to grow a garden and plant beautiful fruit trees that I would see come into fruit distant years from now. I had always dreamed of owning a house instead of renting. But my ex-husband and I had just lived from day to day, low wages, both paying our way through university, broken-down cars, debts...life. However, I had that dream. So I started looking at old, cheap little houses. But trying to afford to buy even a tiny, rundown house still seemed impossible, especially on my own and owning a business where money can be very fluctuating and not guaranteed. It seemed impossible, but I just couldn't put away my dream. Then one day, I saw it! An old 1970s fishing shack close to the water. It was cheap and in terrible condition inside and out. But I could see its potential and value beyond the obvious need for hard work. I could see it being my home. I approached my local bank where I had my business accounts, with excitement, fear and enthusiasm bursting from my naive little soul. I set up an appointment to apply for a mortgage loan. I sat down at the mahogany office desk facing the loans manager, who also happened to the bank manager as it was a small community bank. I nervously said I wanted to inquire about the possibility of getting a mortgage loan and wanted to start my application ASAP as I had found my perfect house. I handed over my business financials.

He glanced at my paperwork momentarily. 'Partner? Husband? You need to show me his financials as well.'

I shook my head, nausea coiling in my stomach. 'No, just me. I want to buy the house by myself.'

He stifled a smile. 'I'm sorry, but a woman on her own, working in her own business, so not even having the stability of permanent employment? Forget it. I'm sorry but there is no way we would even consider looking at an application for a loan.'

I straightened my shoulders and held in tears of disappointment. 'I see. Well, what would I need for the bank to consider looking at my financials? What sort of earnings and deposit potentially are we talking about to get me over the line?'

He shook his head and shrugged. 'I'm sorry, but we just wouldn't consider it. Maybe try one of the big banks. This is a small community bank. We just can't take on this type of risk. I'm sorry, it's not an option.'

I thanked him for his time and left, disappointment and embarrassment swirling through me. I sat in the car to have a little cry, the meeting was over in less than three minutes. I set up loan appointments with all the other banks. I got the same general response from all of them. A woman on her own, running a small business is too risky. One mortgage manager halfheartedly ran a mock loan inquiry with my financials, mainly to humor me and get me out of his office faster, I think.

He pointed at his computer. 'Look, honestly your earnings are not a problem. But the risks of a woman in a new business and applying on your own are disqualifying you from the application process in the system. It's just not viable financially.'

A couple of the loan managers had suggested I approach a financial adviser because sometimes financial mortgage brokers can get loan applications through that banks couldn't. So I set up an appointment with a respected financial broker recommended by a trusted friend. The broker told me bluntly that there was no way I could get a mortgage loan approved in my circumstances and he was surprised I had managed to get any of the banks to even consider running my figures even as a mock application.

Next time I went into the local community bank to deposit my weekly business earnings, the bank manager poked his head out of his office.

He said, 'How did you go with your mortgage application? Did you try the bigger banks?'

I nodded. 'Yes, same answer as you. Too risky.'

He sighed. 'I'm sorry I couldn't help you. Maybe in the future.'

I continued to deposit my business earning in person twice per week in that bank branch. I got on a first name basis with all the staff and the bank manager. My perfect little dream cottage near the water was sold to someone else. I began reading books and doing courses on property investment techniques. I kept looking for a little old cottage to buy. I kept dreaming of owning my own place. Week in, week out, I kept depositing my business earnings into that local bank, always in person twice a week without fail, building friendship and mutual trust with all of the staff and the bank manager. I referred my customers to them. I referred other business owners and property investors I knew through my business and through my property investing courses and property networks. Everyone I referred to the bank, I told them to ask for the bank manager by name. I gave the bank staff discount vouchers for my business, so some of the bank staff became my customers. I opened my business in a second location to negate some of the risks. I continued to work my guts out, growing and promoting my two businesses. By that stage word-of-mouth recommendations from satisfied customers were organically growing my businesses really well too. About five months later, another little, old fishing cottage came up for sale. Cheap, dilapidated, it needed even more hard work than the original one I had fallen in love with. It was located right near the water. I made an offer on that little cottage and my offer was immediately accepted. I gathered my financials, my courage, my property investing knowledge, some supporting documents and my determination. I made an appointment for a mortgage loan application at the local community bank again. When I sat down at that big mahogany office desk the bank manager smiled.

He said, 'We have been here before.'

I said, 'I have my sights set on another cottage.'

He raised a brow. 'I see. I would like to be able to help. Do you have a partner now?'

I shook my head. 'No, still applying for the loan on my own. But I have made some changes. I now have two businesses to negate risks. If I ever have financial issues with one business I have a second business to fall back on. Also the price of this house makes it positively geared. If I rented it out the amount of rental income would more than cover the monthly mortgage repayment and give me extra money on top. So even if both my businesses failed I can rent out the property and that would cover loan repayments, again, minimizing the bank's risks in potential worst case scenarios. Here are rental analysis figures from three real estate agents showing expected minimal rental figures. I will be doing cosmetic renovations on the property immediately which will instantly increase the value and rental potential by approximately 10%-20%. So worst case scenario, if I defaulted on the loan and the bank felt it necessary to seize the property, the resale value would more than cover the mortgage amount borrowed, negating the bank's overall risks if the worse possible scenario occurred. This property's sale price is undervalued. Here are the figures of surrounding property sales in the last twelve months indicating how undervalued the cottage is for its location by the water. So the property already has equity. I already have had an offer accepted at this price. Here is a curbside valuation to show the current market worth. I feel you should consider looking at a mortgage loan application for me this time. I would greatly appreciate the opportunity of having my loans with your bank. As a local business owner I want to help strengthen our community, so I prefer to support a local community bank. As one of your loyal customers, I have all my business and personal accounts with you because I know and trust your business and your staff. Your bank is my preference, before I approach the other banks.'

The bank manager was sitting up in his chair, listening. He extended his hand to take all my financials and said, 'Let's start a loan application. We will see if the approval figures are doable. I will do my best to help you with this loan. No promises, but let's try.'

He ran all my figures. The financials were approved by the skin of my teeth. But my risks as a small business owner and solo woman were too high. I would also have needed an extra $13,800 more in my deposit amount. And I would need it in the next 48 hours to seal the deal with that accepted offer on the cottage.

The bank manager said, 'If you can earn that $13,800 in the next day or so then I will put your loan application through to head office to consider. It may still fail due to the potential risk of your circumstances, but we can try. The bank wont accept you borrowing, lending or being given the extra $13,800 because that amount will then be considered as extra personal debt which will disqualify your borrowing capacity. You need to earn it in your businesses somehow so the bank can see the paper trail of exactly where it has come from.'

Oh, how the hell was I going to pull this off, $13,800 in 48 hours?

I came up with a plan. If 230 of my customers each gave me $60 I would have that $13,800 extra deposit amount I needed. I pulled out my customer list and my phone. I called my most loyal, regular customers first. I said, 'I have an offer going for today only. If you buy one treatment ($60) you get one free. There is no expiry date, you can use it whenever you want. The catch is, you have to pay for it over the phone now to get the deal.'

'Is this to cover speeding fines, Lee?' That was my first customer's response.

I chuckled. *Oh, this was going to be a long day.* 'You know me well, but no, it's not for speeding fines. I'm trying to buy a house and I need extra in my deposit to get my loan approved. So I am running this deal.'

'Good on you. If it's for purchasing a house, then I will buy ten. That should do me for a years worth of treatments.'

Wow! My customers were incredibly supportive and I got my extra $13,800 in 48 hours along with a hoarse throat from all the phone calls. The bank manager was astonished, apparently he had not expected me to earn the extra cash in two days, but he put my loan application through as promised. The loan was at first declined by head office and the bank manager went into bat for me and managed to get it approved as an 'in branch' application. I bought my little dream cottage by the water. I did those cosmetic improvements and it is still my home today. We pick fresh fruit to eat and make jams and chutneys, from those fruit trees I planted in my garden, just like I dreamed. Not only that, to all those banks who told me to forget about trying to buy a house as a single, solo woman owning a small business, well, I went on to purchase two more investment properties to grow my property portfolio in the following five years as a solo woman and a business owner. I used equity leverage that I created doing up my little cottage home. And my businesses that the banks would not consider financially stable enough to even attempt a loan application, well those businesses have run successfully for over twenty years. About a decade later I did end up falling in love again and remarried. We are looking at buying an investment property together, which will make it five properties we have as my husband owned a house too. If the purchase goes ahead it will be the first time I buy a property jointly rather than purchasing by myself as a solo woman, who owns her own business.

Moral of the story, if someone tells you that you can't, don't believe them. If everyone tells you that you can't, still don't believe them.

~ 60 ~

I danced on every street corner
that had a street lamp flickering
and pretended I was at a disco

Old farmhouse

I am thinking of where I grew up
I would love to be there again
Walking through the paddocks
rye grass up past my thighs
the sun, a paler shade of winter
making the ghost gums
a vivid white
in the afternoon haze.
The cows move slow
as they graze their way
through the distant paddocks
and fresh cut hay.
The breeze smells like the earth and trees
fashioned from their warm embrace
March flies drone through the tangled undergrowth
through the ferns and wildflowers
My dog barks and smells the breeze
bounds away through the swaying trees
hot on the heels of a springing hare
dashing through the ferns and maidenhair
I hear her barking ringing clear
echoing through the valley and cliffs so sheer
I turn towards home in the dying light

My dog bounds back to walk at my side
up the long drive, past the old dairy sheds
past kangaroos eating grass, magpies watching overhead
Along the rough track well-trod and dusty
in through the iron gate well-used and rusty
vines curling up through the fence posts and wire
I hear laughter and voices round the warm wood fire
our sturdy old farmhouse, worn wood and old stone
The familiar welcoming feel of home...

....So far away from the traffics drone
the computer screen and the ringing phone
My mind and feet firmly planted back
on level 5, apartment 3
out my window, the sprawl of pulsing Sydney inner city
I smile to myself at my moment of nostalgia
but deep down I know, in my heart will always be
a little place where the rye grass stretches free
and the sun on the paddocks beckons me

~ 62 ~

While I dance to the rhythm of my own heartbeat
you walk in and knock me off my feet

~ 63 ~

Let's cuddle puddle in the sun

~ 64 ~

I don't take orders, sorry. I follow my heart, my guts and my female intuition and right now they are saying a big, fat NO

~ 65 ~

Rising

Tossing and turning
rising to what we are born to be
stretching comfortably into authenticity
Women of the earth, of the rolling waves
women of the forests, the savannas
the ancient mountains
lovers of animals and nature
Hearts and hands of mothers and healers
Carving our way through deep paths
through lush forests, pulsing cities
high mountains, thirsty deserts
with the pulse of our own truth
thundering through our veins.
With achievements, hurts, defenses and passions
cracked opened and accepted and loved

Choosing those who walk beside us
for the light of realness
and kindness in their eyes and hearts
walking with the strength
of those who have been there and back
and lived it with resilience
Speaking with the gentleness

and wisdom of being in the fire
and not shriveling
letting it burn away the lies
ignite truth and freedom

We are dancing our warrior woman's call
and certainly don't need approval to do so
We are walking our spirit woman
and living every piece of our hearts
Dancing warrior women
under this deep blue stretch of sky
with love, with gratefulness, with brightness
with each other

~ 66 ~

Sometimes, I am just not capable of pretending
to listen to your annoying, logical, good advice

~ 67 ~

I packed my heart
away on the shelf
she is waiting there
for a day with bluer skies

Mother Nature

Blue birthing waters
across the earth
as nature sighs
in labored birth
pushing up the trees
and breathing out the sky
the oceans in her palms
the mountains her eye
A maiden in her evergreen dress of leaves
Wise old woman of the winter freeze

Mother of a thousand moods

Wind stung waves on a restless ocean
the silver sparkle of a stream's swift motion
A lone bird in distant flight
the silver moon in the sky at night
Dappled sun on blowing grains
the pounding rhythm of flooding rains

Mother of a thousand moods
Leaping kangaroo, silver trout
parched land in a harsh drought

A lazy lizard, the dingo's low howl
singing wrens, the hoot of an owl
Raging storms, bushfire gloom
the simple truth of a flower in bloom

Mother of a thousand moods

She is a beast with tooth and claw
pale our eyes with visions raw
She is the still that comes quietly
peacefully into our souls
and makes them breathe

~ 69 ~

Lost words

I pick my heart up off the floor
like it is merely a dropped teacup
pretend I can brush off the damage
I may do no good
but I will do no harm
I clutch at my courage
like it is a rope around my throat
say the words I need to say
stand up and speak my truth
While you have got one hand resting on my heart
and the other gripping my jugular
I wait
while you decide which one you will squeeze.
Forgiveness takes her time.
Help me find my feet
forgiveness
And you surge to your feet
let the cards fall to the floor
walk out
to go and lose yourself
in the bottle.
I break.

~ 70 ~

Sure, I can be a graceful, feminine badass simultaneously
just watch me

~ 71 ~

Heartbreaks
reveal truth
and clarity
to help you
stumble on
true love
in time

~ 72 ~

I'm a wild hair woman. Only other wild hair women
know what I'm talking about.

~ 73 ~

When dementia took her mind
It broke my heart
every day
as she forgot my birthday
then forgot my name
and forgot she ever had a daughter
It broke my heart
in a million ways
till I realized
though her mind was gone
in her heart
she is still the kind, sweet, gentle
most beautiful mother in the world

~ 74 ~

Your smile
does something
so beautiful
to my soul

Take a moment

Take a moment and be still
notice the beauty close at hand
reach out and touch the earth
feel the wholeness of the land
Treasure the breath of seasons turning
notice the beautiful blue sky
look at the life unfolding around you
it isn't hard if you will try
The laugh of a child
the smile of a friend or a stranger
love shared in a family
music, kindness, laughter,
all of the gifts given for free
a singing bird, the sighing wind
warm sunlight dancing on the sea

Nurture your passions
if the shadows are long
listen to the rhythm
of your hearts own song
Stand up, stay true, be kind
take a hold of your dreams
and let them shine

Whether the skies in your life
are grey or blue
take a moment and be still
take a moment to truly love, *you*
Treasure the breath of life's seasons turning
take each sunrise as a sign
to live, truly, deeply, fiercely
to pick up courage and joy
and leave fear and doubt behind

Remember, it is the rain
that makes flowers bloom
in the wild, vast seasons
of your heart
So pick the wildflowers
from the wilderness of your soul
weave them into a wreath for your hair

Take a moment and be still
notice the beauty close at hand
reach out and touch the earth
feel the wholeness of the land
Seize each passing day with love
nurture your heart to understand
each new day, each hour, each breath
we hold a million treasures in our hand.

~ 76 ~

I roamed
so many maps
to finally find
myself

~ 77 ~

Sometimes we are fierce, unrelenting, all or nothing, powerful
women, and darling, we couldn't care less if you don't like it

Australian Boab
(Adansonia gregorii)

Red moon

Deep
speaks to me in colors
fills my bleeding pen
notes from my soul
tumble out easily

Home
I hear her voice calling
speaks of hills that ache
with familiar voices, faces
in a field where sunlight dances
on ripened grain and mountain lakes
It is where you are waiting, where my heart is home

I picture you with the wind in your hair
the miles stretch out from here
I pushed you too far, but you stood still
We talked about love, and you just knew
I gazed at the stars, and you flew
Love, I'm aching to hold you
under the light of this red moon

~ 79 ~

At one point I decided
I should try to be responsible
Yeah, that didn't work out

~ 80 ~

A healthy diet is not just about what you eat,
it is also about sharing meals with those you care about
in beautiful places, among music, laughter and love.

~ 81 ~

If I ever meet Murphy I'm going to
poke him in the eye, him and his stupid laws

Old friend (full version)

Old friend, come sit a while
it is all out on the table between us
I reach for your hand
let my heart fall out on my sleeve
despite the miles and the hard years
between us is something beautiful
I let go of everything
smile at your gypsy heart
it belongs to the wide blue sky.
Always did

We are driving away
heading north up the coast
Bundaberg, Rocky, Cairns and The Cape
then across the red center
where the heartlands ache
and The Dreaming weaves Songlines
through the vast landscape
Our lives packed in our bags
just our guitars
and a pocketful of rhymes
leaving the rest far behind

There is a fierce peace out here
on the empty road
carried in on the dry winds
this freedom makes some sort of sense
Dry heat and the desert speaks
of vast horizons and endless possibilities
Our hearts float away
on the summer breeze
Open minds and held hands
we make our paths
through these ancient lands
holding just the things that are meaningful

Old friend, come sit a while
it is all out on the table between us
I reach for your hand
let my heart fall out on my sleeve
despite the miles and the hard years
between us is something beautiful
I let go of everything
smile at your gypsy heart
it belongs to the wide blue sky
Always did.

Now the shadows are long
and my hair has turned grey
My feet walked many paths
and found their way
As the years slipped past
and I traveled far
became older, wiser, kinder
When the way was not clear
or the addictions, demons, heartbreaks

laid me wasted
it was you, old friend
no matter how far
strumming softly on that old guitar
strumming softly to my heart
The rock I could never tame
it was always you
who could find my heart

Echinacea, Coneflower
(Echinacea Purpurea & Angustifolia)

~ 83 ~

Let go
you are meant
to get wet
dancing
in the rain.
Life is messy
and beautiful

~ 84 ~

Oh, is that you tripping over my boundaries again?

Kangaroo Paw
(Anigozanthos)
Australian Native

Medicine women's ancient wisdom

Golden Wattle
(Acacia Pycnantha)
Australian Native
flowering in late spring
& early winter
Traditional medicine
for colds, flu, laryngitis

Modern non-utopia

Where is the love, the solidarity, unity?
What will we choose, while we still have a choice
a planet full of life, or a pocket full of money?
Extinct bees, no more honey?
Political corruption, scandals, lies
global wide
wildfires
glaciers melt in global warming
mining agreements flourish
as mother nature screams her warning
we drill deeper and deeper into her veins
while the ancient forests burn
and the seasons change their turn
and the sacred sights fall into mining legislation.

World wide fear, locked down nations
first world obesity, third world starvation
Gay rights, economies shatter, black lives matter?
Where is the solidarity, the kindness?
Where is the truth?
We look to the sky
and wonder why
and wonder if we could

but rarely ask if we should
Where is the love? I don't feel it
What is the truth? I don't hear it
Dying people, plants, animal species
Our mother, the earth, is crying
her body is raped and she is dying
What if we speak the truth?
What if we face the truth?
It is not a mystery, let's change history
solidarity, unity.
Let's choose a future
Choose life *full of honey*

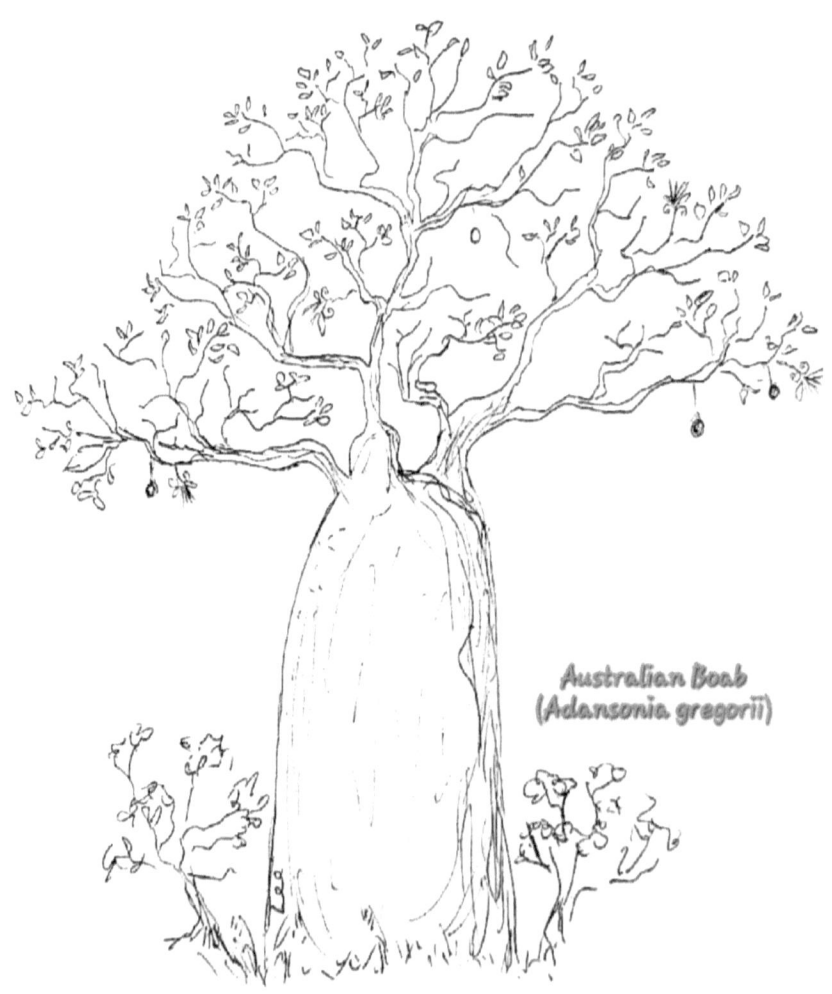

Australian Boab
(Adansonia gregorii)

~ 86 ~

Difficult questions, bare feet and hugs
are welcome at the picnic

~ 87 ~

Strong is
looking out
the window
of a broken heart
past the
cracked glass
and still
seeing
a beautiful
world

Golden Everlasting Daisy
(Asteraceae)
Australian Native
fliwers in spring, summer, autumn

Pilgrim

I've been roaming on so many maps
thought I might lose my mind
but, in fact, I found so many pieces
of myself, that I had left behind
Found my feet on the cobblestone streets of London
and it felt like home

Felt my heart come back, and open up a crack
dancing in Dublin in the arms of an Irishman
he held me tight and kissed me deep
as we said goodbye under a flickering lamp
on that misty Dublin street
then I ran to catch a plane, bound for Paris and dreams

Among the palaces, cafes, bridges and faces
I'm sure I found my spirit in one of those places
among the fashion, The Metro, the attitude, the art
as is the custom I tied my heart
to the Pont des Arts bridge
and I threw away the key
Every step I took, I smiled so wide
and knew my soul was free

As I breathed in the history and tranquility of ancient Rome
connected to the culture and completely found my own
I gazed out from the top of Vesuvius
far below to the Aegean Sea
trying to spot a mermaid on the Island of Capri
Strung my heart on the line
traveled enough maps to find
in every street and corner
a reason for my soul to love and dance
and sing forever

~ 89 ~

An angel rocked up in faded jeans and an old Nirvana t-shirt, he had a three day growth and the mountains in his eyes. Sometimes, we meet angels whose wings we can not see. Ordinary people who wander into our life and are there for us no matter what and do so much more than you or anyone would ever expect. People who run towards danger to protect others. He was supposed to be on holidays, a well deserved break spending time with family. But the emergency lines were so busy he had rushed to the scene, with no time to put on his SES emergency rescue suit.

It was all going splendidly until I tangoed down the wrong fork
in the road and fell flat on my shimmying little patootie

Xanthorrhoea

Missing

I can't help but dream for more
little house on a distant beach
sunrise on a quiet shore
I can't help but dream so wide
I think I'm on your side
shared soft whispers and held hands
make a wish on distant stars
should I leave it to the tides
is the weather not just right
for you to sail to my side tonight?

White lace on a day covered in smiles
white chiffon second time round
seems so far away
Let my mind just slip away
try to make the grey skies turn blue
and believe that dreams come true
White curtains looking out
on a back yard
full of dreams
children
laughter

and the man, with the ocean in his eyes
and a heart of gold
he seems so far away
with every day that grows old
My mind is full of doubt
but still I dream so wide
I think I'm calling
I think I'm falling
I think I'm learning
to trust life's seasons.
I'll just leave it to the tide
to bring him to my side

Kangaroo Paw
(Anigozanthos)
Australian Native

~ 92 ~

How to irritate your neighbors, children, partner

1. Go into your garden, pick five or six strong blades of grass

2. Place one blade of grass between your two thumbs, clasp your fingers to make a grass whistle

3. Blow on the grass whistle, ensuring you make the loudest possible squeaking sounds

4. The longer and louder, the better. Walk the perimeter of your garden and through all rooms in your house, blowing your grass whistle as loud as you can. Ensure you have the spare blades of grass in your pocket to replace used grass or in case someone tries to confiscate the grass.

There are two types of people in the world, people who look at you strangely for dancing along the beach and people who kick off their shoes and join in. Always go for option B people.

Eucalyptus /Gum tree
(Eucalypteae)

~ 94 ~

I am only one step away
from completely losing it and telling you
what an egotistical, chauvinistic, misogynistic,
sexist, racist, moronic, clueless, narrow-sighted,
narrow-minded dumb git you are being sometimes humanity

~ Mother Nature

~ 95 ~

Medicine women

Women, sisters, a call of the heart
a call to seek our wisdom passed
and on and on, by word of mouth
it travels the years vast
Opening minds to a truth
a way, a pattern, a path
and each time hands unfold
kinetic healing retold
balance restored
and felt by yet another
to fill a dark place
weaken or strengthen
or willingly give up strength
to mend another

As I reach to pluck a leaf, or root or flower
and with my hands and mind
harvest it to yield the healing power
I am awed by the abundant gifts
Mother Earth bestows for free
and profoundly honored
that she lends some to me

~ 96 ~

I am mostly a calm, peaceful, responsible woman
except the parts of me that say, screw it, let's go wild

~ 97 ~

Find the rhythms
that liberate your soul
and dance them
uninhibited
untamed
Find languages that are universal
and speak them.
Find love that is universal
and spread it

~ 98 ~

Hell yes, I'm up for being single, independent and fabulous

~ 99 ~

When all is said & done

When all is said and done, my love
and our life and love flickers dim
our hands were held, clutched,
trembling at times
but were held fast none the less

You have spread my wings in blue skies of love
deep and free and wide
and in a breath too
you have crushed them at times
to tumble drown and die
I've held you in my arms as the sunlight faded
and bowed out to the waning moon
Lost deep in your eyes
under wide summer skies
flushed with a thousand stars

I have screamed my pain at your tear stained face
spanked your heart till it is black and blue
I have lost myself in your deep embrace
loved and lived far more deep and true
I've been messy and real and wrong and right
learned my fair share of lessons at your hand

learned resilience, self-reliance, authenticity
learned to listen and understand.
Your gentle hand has caressed my face
with kind, warm love
You have stood by me, and faced the fire
in moments when our paths trod true
you have left me cold, and beaten too
lying crumpled and falling apart
torn deep at your absent heart

I have quietened my voice and found my gentleness
dimmed my fire to let your soul shine
We have held each other's hearts, like torn silk
woven, threadbare, in love
I've laughed so hard with your wit and playfulness
rolled deep in your passion and fire
I have fallen in love with you a million times
laughed endlessly and loved true
felt blessed at the magic we share
and the way my heart sings at your side
danced our vows in the summer heat
danced in white as your love-struck bride
Long years in your arms, my heart felt home
long beach walks with you by my side

I have shattered like glass
as you crawled to the bottle
love wilted like dying flowers
beaten, empty, scarred deep by the fight
But we've found in these dark hours
much greater strength and clarity
than we could ever have found in the light

When all is said and done, my love
and the light and dark roads are all through
I will hold my grace and truth either way
because I have chosen to
Though the path at times has been hard, my friend
when all is said and done
from those twists and turns and highs and lows
we have loved far more deep and true
we have danced and screamed and run
we have fallen and flown and we've made it through
when all is said and done.

How to find a mermaid at the beach

1) Put on your bikini or swimsuit and grab a towel.

2) Go to the beach and paddle into the waves.

3) Imagine you are a mermaid. (*Oh, you just found a mermaid.*)

4) Look around. If there are other women swimming, smile and wave at them and imagine they are mermaids too.

Golden Everlasting Daisy
(Asteraceae)
Australian Native
flowers in spring, summer, autumn

Medicine women's traditional wisdom

Manuka Tea Tree / Manuka Myrtle
(Leptospermum Scoparium)

Native to New Zealand and south east Australia. Flowers in Spring & Summer. Medicinal properties: leaves are anti-inflammatory, antimicrobial, treat respiratory infections, colds, flu. Bark is used externally to treat skin conditions. Nectar produces Manuka honey. The honey has been used since ancient times as a topical treatment for healing wounds, skin infections and as a powerful antibacterial. Medically, it effectively treats Staphylococcus the major wound-infecting types of bacteria. Helps Strep throat, treats wounds, burns, skin ulcers, diabetic wounds, stomach ulcers, gastric problems, abdominal pain, Irritable Bowel Syndrome (IBS), Inflammatory Bowel Disease (IBD), gingivitis, tooth plaque & bacterial shingles.

~ 101 ~

THE NAMES PAGE
(You will know what it is about by the end)

Lee Maywood
4/4/2025

Online

Could I buy these three new dresses
they are 50% off, online
but you have to buy all three
then you get the fourth one for free
Could you pick us up at midnight
Could you pick us up right now
Could you drop me around the corner
I can't walk, it's just too far
Can I borrow the car
Can I borrow your credit card
Can I borrow this dress
I can't clean up my mess!
Can you drop me to school
I don't want to catch the bus
I don't like bread
I don't like fruit
I don't like snacks
I don't like nuts
I don't like salad
I don't like meat, much
I will have to buy my school lunch
I don't have anything to wear
Oh god, I hate my hair

Everyone is wearing
their skirts this short
I don't like the one you bought
I don't care
It's not fair
I don't want to share
There won't be any alcohol there
it's just a tiny party
I don't like that
Can we get a cat?
What would you know
Why can't I go
It wasn't me
Don't blame me
I hate that jacket
the top of your arms look like they wobble
My phone is over two years old
I need the newest model
I lost my house keys
I hate the smell of cheese
I need a new phone
PLEASE!
That's stupid
That's not funny
That's dumb
I need more money
Besides last week, I haven't bought clothes in ages...

They are such a delight, teenagers

~ 103 ~

I generally avoid temptation, unless it has to do with chocolate, spontaneous ocean dips, spontaneous dancing, holidays, music festivals, travel, ice cream, road trips, sleeping in, singing in the shower, singing in the car, singing in the living room, cuddling animals, driving too damn fast, riding motorbikes, climbing mountains, laughing so much my face and stomach hurt for the following few days, overindulging in mangoes, trekking in Nepal, trips to Paris, picnics with girlfriends, mosh pit enthusiasm, dancing all night, playing with dogs, surfing badly... and a bunch of other things.

~ 104 ~

Heart   break
The blood on my hands
from your broken heart
makes me ache
everyday
still

~ 105 ~

When I roam the world
I open my mind
when I sit still with someone
I open my heart

Moments of mayhem, magic & mundane

I stare at his tall form silhouetted against the windows
It doesn't seem to matter what the annoying git does
I have always had this endless capacity
to adore him, regardless.
Blue skies and sunshine filter in
from the opened window behind him
the smell of spring is in the air and the sound of surf
Salt trails from the waves
have settled on his shoulders and chest as usual
I should be angry, I should be furious
I should be telling him off
But instead, I've been laughing hysterically
that unstoppable humor tumbling from his soul
tangles me in the magic of the moment
makes my heart sing, my inner child dance
and I forget I'm anything but in love
Damn him and his silliness and wit
sweeping me off my feet
when I was going to make a stand
when I planned to be furious
Moments of mayhem, magic, and mundane
I should know better.

~ 107 ~

Home

I hear her voice calling
speaks of hills that ache
with familiar voices, faces
a field where sunlight dances
on ripened grain and mountain lakes
It is where you are waiting, where my heart is home

Raising

From birth
what if we taught our daughters
to wrestle
to fix things
to train in martial arts?
To be confident with strength
and power, like we do our sons.

What if instead of showing our girls
to choose pretty clothes
apply makeup
walk in high heels
we encouraged them
with the freedom
the expectation
that they become
fierce
warriors
activists
engineers
leaders
What if we liberated our girls
right from birth

from an upbringing
that fundamentally creates
and perpetuates objectification
and status dependent on beauty?
We caution our daughters from the start
be careful
avoid danger.
What if instead we told them
you are fierce, strong, resourceful, unstoppable

What if our daughters were taught to be Amazons,
advocates for justice, warriors for nature,
to become leaders of the heart,
inventors of clean technologies,
black belts in martial arts
long before they became objectifications
of beauty and society.

What if our daughters could recognize danger
and easily conquer it
instead of the need to be careful or afraid
and avoid potential dangers?
What if we made the world
less dangerous for our daughters
That is the smell of true freedom my sisters.
Why create victims, instead of warriors?

A question,
what makes high heels and makeup beautiful?
More beautiful than strong, fit, and resourceful?
In truth
it is social conditioning
stemming in part from commercialism

They can sell shoes and makeup and fashion
and sell beauty do they ever
They can't sell
strong, fierce, or powerful
and it is harder to CONTROL

Is perpetuating such social cycles
truly what we want as women?
Or in truth is it just what suits
those who line their pockets
from this so called 'beauty'
that we so readily buy in little bottles
and wrap ourselves in
to face the world
What if we treated our daughters
the *same* as our sons
and what if we teach our sons from birth
to admire strength and wit
instead of beauty?

And in the same way we teach our daughters
that men are strong and can be dangerous
what if we taught our sons
that women are strong and can be dangerous
and what if all women were?
What if we liberated our girls
right from birth
from an upbringing
that fundamentally creates objectification
and status dependent on beauty
And the mental and physical torment that goes with it
for years, sometimes for a lifetime
for women, young and old

...Is my hair OK? Is my makeup OK? Is this dress OK?
Are these shoes OK?
I look fat.
You can't wear that.
Lose weight, count calories, lose the attitude
You are too tall / too short / too thin / too fat / to wear that.
You are too loud, too quiet, not good enough,
not pretty enough, not strong enough
Don't eat that. Don't do that. Don't say that.
Don't wear that,
it makes you look too fat / too short / too flat.
You can just wear a hat
or a scarf to cover the grey regrowth
I'll wear a jacket to hide my waist / my hips / my arms
Wear this! It is slimming!
Don't say that. Don't be like that.
These shoes hurt my feet, but they look beautiful
It doesn't really fit. If I lose weight, I can fit this.
Lose weight, fix your hair.
Your boobs aren't the right size, neither is your butt
nor your waist or hips, or legs, or nose or lips
they need to be bigger, smaller, thinner, larger
God, I look terrible, I need makeup.
That is too bright / too short / doesn't suit you /
makes you look old /not dressy enough /
not good enough...

How much inequality and lack of worth
do we unwittingly create from birth
in both genders
in our daily words and actions
instilling a sense of gender difference, worthlessness

and inequality
instead of instilling understanding and appreciation
of different strengths and connections?

What if we truly noticed and analyzed
how much our social conditioning
related to upbringing
instills and perpetuates gender inequality
objectification
and both cultural and social acceptance
of these traits in our children
What if we focused on instilling
a sense of worthiness and confidence
What if we truly instilled equality right from birth?
Instead of just marching for it as adults.

When was the last time
you did something with your daughter
to make her feel or look beautiful?
When was the last time
you did something with your daughter
to make her feel strong and powerful and unstoppable?
And do those odds stack up at all?

~ 109 ~

She wore her courage
like wings
and I fell deep
into her blue skies

Echinacea, Coneflower
(Echinacea Purpurea &
Angustifolia)
Native to prairies of eastern,
central and northern America.
Flowering in summer, use of
roots all year round.
Traditional medicinal uses
include external application for
insect bites, burns, wounds,
chewing the roots for treating
throat and tooth infections and
internal use for cough, pain,
snake bites, stomach cramps
and enhancing immunity,
respitory infections, also a
powerful antioxident.

~ 110 ~

I have had great success at being ridiculous

~ 111 ~

Wild knowing

In the distance, not too far
is a different type of emptiness
wide spaces, wild knowing
freedom, authenticity
women of the earth, of the forests, of the sea
a calling of the heart
as it opens
flutters free
into the wide blue skies
fluttering like red butterflies
playful, beautiful, free
wild knowing
free spirit

~ 112 ~

My husband

I sank deep into Eden with you
You plucked at strings in my soul
like you were playing a harp
icy fingers playing my darkness
warm fingers playing my light
when you held my hand the world would stop a moment

We called it love
We called it soulmates
We called it
deep in our hearts and bones
your mind, drawing endless laughter
from my lips
My mind, my heart
falling endlessly in love with you
over and over
unstoppable
as the water flowing down the slopes
of those mountains
where we often roamed
You, with your arm around my waist
tight
pulling me close to the side of your body

where I could feel your warmth
smell your aftershave
feel bits of our bodies bump together
as we walked in time
my fingers laced through yours
like woven tapestry

I left you chained to the poison

addiction
with a head full of denial
nothing could save you
Never dreamed it would kill you
Never dreamed no one would ever
get a chance to say goodbye
Your death struck such horror in my soul
They told me autopsies
are done with deep respect
as I howled down the phone
sitting in the car park
listening to the autopsy doctor's respectful voice
calmly describe the causes of your death
scientifically
respectfully
Your death struck such horror in my soul
The only thing I could do
was change forever
Let every piece of who I was before
seep out of the cracks in my broken heart
like a darkness thicker than night
Nothing is gonna save me now
but a crucible of evolution

~ 113 ~

I take time
to smell the roses
that you picked
for me
from our garden

~ 114 ~

I walked slowly
along the sand
and fell in love
with the crashing waves

~ 115 ~

I may look politely interested on the outside, but inside I stopped listening to your regurgitated, self-righteous monologue about 5 seconds after you started talking

Medicine women's ancient wisdom

Eucalyptus / Gum Tree
(Eucalypteae Eucalyptus various)
An Australian native with over 700 species. Medicinal properties: antibacterial, anti-inflammatory, analgesic, antifungal, bronchodilator, antioxidant, immune stimulant. Treats respiratory infection, lung inflammation, enhances respiratory function generally. A natural pain reliever beneficial for reducing rheumatoid arthritis pain. Powerful antibacterial, antiviral, antifungal properties makes it an excellent cleanser. Topically used as antiseptic for cuts and bruises and promotes faster healing. The essential oil promotes relaxation, mental clarity, reduces anxiety improves mood, energy and has calming properties.

Eucalyptus /Gum tree
(Eucalypteae)

Blue bikini

I lost my blue bikini
I really don't know how
it seemed so fitted and strong
I don't know what went wrong
But *poof!* Suddenly it was gone
It wasn't gone a little way
it vanished out of sight
like a torpedo through the waves
it darted away from me
into the ocean's heaving depths
deep, deep into the sea

I floundered about, I dove deep
I searched high and low
but no matter what I did
that blue bikini hid
Perhaps it got gobbled by a silver fish
or caught under a rock
Maybe a shark started choking on it
then coughed it onto the dock
Maybe it caught on an old man's fishing line
and gave him a nasty shock
or perhaps a sailor found it

and wore it under a frock
Maybe it sunk so deep it found a pirate's treasure chest
or possibly the wind blew it high into a booby's nest
perhaps it was pounded on the rocks
lying lost, forlorn, torn and frayed
or maybe the ocean took it
to give to a mermaid

I really cant be sure
it is an enigmatic mystery
But my main concern, besides needing a martini
was the busy beach
where I had to walk without my blue bikini
So I walked ashore, my head held high
pretending nothing happened
through the families having picnics
and the lifeguards on the sand
Past the trendy city folk
in G-strings with fake tan
Past the couple waving flags and dreadlocks
who looked like protesting tree-huggers
past the politician jogging nimbly in tiny red budgie smugglers
(Who I wished I didn't have to face)
Oh, I walked by them all with such poise
such deportment, such grace

~ 117 ~

We imagined
music
as we fell
in love
slow dancing
on the
cracked pavement

~ 118 ~

I have a lot of growing up to do

~ 119 ~

Yarn about nature's wisdom

When I was studying naturopathy and nutrition, one of the first things we learned in herbal medicine was *The Doctrine of Signatures.* It is an ancient concept dating back to 40-70 CE. It states that in the wild, medicinal plants often naturally grow where they are needed or resemble the color or shape of the organ or body system they help treat. The concept dates back to Galen and Dioscorides, considered the grandfathers of modern medicine, but the idea was taken from much more ancient tribal medical beliefs. The *Doctrine of Signatures* is widely cataloged in ancient Roman and Greek texts from physicians, botanists, pharmacologists and ancient medical texts such as *De Manteria Medica,* an ancient medical book used for over 1500 years, making it one of the longest lasting pharmacology books of all time. The concept of plants growing where they are needed and resembling the body organs they treat, appears in many ancient medical system all around the world. Some examples of The Doctrine of Signatures in real-life include the following: Wild aloe vera naturally grows in hot, dry desert regions, aloe vera treats sunburn. Wild arnica naturally grows in mountainous regions, arnica treats strains, sprains, broken bones, and internal injuries. Ginseng root looks like the shape of a human body and can be used as a whole body tonic, strengthening all body systems both physically and mentally and enhancing immunity and energy. Hearts-ease violets have the shape of a human heart in the flower petals and were prescribed as a general heart tonic, also for enhancing the adrenal system and to ease emotional pain and grief. Eyebright flowers resemble the shape of a human eye and are effective in treating eye infections, eye strain and strengthening the iris in conditions like glaucoma. These are just a few examples in hundreds.

Nature's healing power, unassuming sense and gentle wisdom is beautiful isn't it? Did you know, if there is a sick tree in a forest surrounding trees try to nurse it back to health by sending nutrients to it's root systems? And trees keep ancient stumps of long felled companions alive for centuries by feeding them a sugar and nutrient solution via the roots. Trees are constantly communicating with each other, sending electrical and chemical signals via fungal networks and will warn each other of danger. As the final act of life, felled and dying trees send out their own nutrients and electrical energy to benefit the health of other trees in the surrounding forest, sacrificing all they have left to help others. In a heartwarming display of loyalty certain birds, for instance Australian galahs and sulpha-crested cockatoos keep the one same mate for life, 80 to 100 years is their potential lifespans together. Male Adelie penguins 'propose' to females by giving her a rock. Otters sleep holding hands with their mate so they don't drift apart in the water at night. Beautiful nature.

~ 120 ~

Mother Nature just called, she said, get your caboose out here girl

Firewood Banksia
(Banksia Menziesii)
Fowering Autumn & Winter

~ 121 ~

Deep blue Pacific Ocean

She curled into the blankets, listening to the crickets and marsh frogs chirping out the window. Deep pink and orange settled across the summer sky. Leaning up on one elbow, she looked across the ryegrass paddocks, a vast shimmering matrix of dew in the dawn light. Rising from bed, she slipped on a bikini and wetsuit, tossed a change of clothes into her backpack. The old wooden stairs creaked as she tiptoed down, grabbing her surfboard she left the house. The cliffs moaned as the winds clawed them, the spear grass bending sideways, thrashing a wild tango around her legs. Walking to the headland, she gazed out across the tattered coastline. Dense bushland lined the edges of long white sandy beaches. In the distance, a fishing trawler chugged towards Sandpiper Bay. Neat rows of cottages painted in seaside pastels and a few small shops clung to the harbour's edge. Speedboats, trawlers and yachts bobbed in the currents by the pier, among a jumble of ropes, fishing nets, cargo and barnacles, gulls circling overhead. Rowdy shouts and laughter of fishermen unloading at the docks hung on the offshore southeasterlies. Surfboard underarm, she followed the dirt track winding through wattle down to the sand. Her green eyes scanned the waves. The swell was high, sea mist swirled at the shoreline.

He always loved the notorious breaks.

He was seventy meters out, thrashing the oversized waves, his wet skin and hair reflecting the golden sunrise. He glided along the crest then wiped-out into the crashing water, surfaced, shook his head, spotted her, and waved. She paddled out, nosed her board left.

'You made it.' He had the look of the ocean in his eyes, sparkling and a little untamed as he smiled at her across the waves.

'Just.' She squinted against the rising sun, leaned forward, flicking wet hair off her face. 'This next set is pumping.' She watched the glassy green wall of water crashing towards them, slid her chest down onto the wet board and started paddling.

The thundering swell took hold, her heart pounded. She leapt to her feet, aware of him riding close on her right side. Speeding through the barrel, she glided her fingers through the blue-green torrents of water arcing overhead, immersed in the roar and colors of the ocean's raw power propelling her forward. She breathed in the speed and salty air moments longer then wiped-out into the swirling currents, pummeled, rolled, tasted salt water, then bobbed up for air.

He surface close by, blinking water out of his eyes and grinning from ear to ear. 'This is the life!'

She grabbed her floating surfboard and pulled it under her torso, eyes on the next wave. 'Absolutely.'

He jutted his chin towards the reef. 'Looked like you almost came undone among the rocks, true adrenaline junkie style, as usual.'

'I was fine,' she lied, heart still racing from the near collision. 'Just living on the edge a little, my friend.'

'One of the many reasons you're the best.' He smirked and raised one brow.

Smug git, knows me too damn well. He wasn't buying it. She tossed her hair defiantly. Growing up together, no one could rein them in. It always felt like them against the world on some wild frontier.

Fighting off the rules, pushing the limits. She remembered how much they used to laugh and vow they would never conform to the institutions. *God, she had missed that nomadic spirit of his these last few years.*

The swell rolled around them deep azure blue, swirling with foam.

She smiled, paddled away towards the next barrel forming. 'Come on, stop flailing around back there.' She yelled over her shoulder.

He laughed, paddling towards her.

~ 122 ~

How to make daisy chains

1) Go walking in the woods, park or meadows

2) Pick daisies and other flowers as you walk

3) Weave flowers into two daisy chains, one for your wrist, one for your hair

4) Frolic and dance through the woods, park or meadows wearing your daisy chains, pretending you are a fairy princess. (This can be done with or without children, friends, lover.)

~ 123 ~

Every day
my heart
speaks to me
more clearly

Trinkets

I wander peaceful
lost in the sunlight
lost in the shoreline
stretching away.
Sinking into the rhythm
the heartbeat of the waves
following the shells, where
the high tide has left them
A million trinkets
laying scattered in the sand
a million little treasures
lovingly carved by
Mother Nature's hand.
Shaped by the caress
of seasons turning
the sun's slow burning
and the endless change of tides
Smoothed by the winds
and the years and the sands
treasures carved
by Mother Nature's loving hands.
Enthralled in the soaring mountain peeks
touched deep by the breeze

and the endless blue sky
this love is ageless and endless and simple.
This love is our souls being part of the earth
this is the love we were made for at birth.

Xanthorrhoea Australis

~ 125 ~

Yet again, I fall flat on my face tripping over the high road

Author's Note

Thank you for reading and sharing some of my stories within these pages. If you have a physical copy of this book, please consider passing it on to another woman/women to read now that you have finished. But first, flick back to the 'Names Page' number 101. Write your name and the date. You will see my name there already. Hopefully, whoever you gift this book to, will in turn, gift it to another woman, for it is through our sharing of stories, experiences and life that we women connect and grow.

Like the ancient flow of tides turning, new seasons stirring
the moon waning, so are the changing seasons of life
connecting women in friendship, strength and shared wisdom
as beautiful and perennial as the flowers growing wild
in the meadows. On and on through women's hands and hearts
we share our stories, our joys, our heartbreaks, our victories
our experiences, our love. We support and uplift each other
as our sisters have done for countless years before.

Lee Maywood

Author Bio

Lee Maywood is an Australian author and illustrator. She lives on the south coast in Jervis Bay area, after growing up in the Southern Highlands. Lee writes in fiction, non-fiction and auto-biographical genres, including children's picture books, upmarket speculative thrillers, poetic literary collections, health and wellness guides. Her studies included a Bachelor of Health Science in Complementary Medicine, an Advanced Diploma of Naturopathy, Nutrition and Oriental Medicine, Certificates in Oncology Support and Remedial Therapies, Permaculture Design, Conservation and Real Estate Investing. Lee spent 25 years as a health practitioner and business owner, specializing in the treatment of chronic pain and injuries. She retired from her profession in the health industry and now focuses on her other lifelong passions of writing, permaculture gardening, native wildlife and creating free uplifting community events. Lee Maywood's love of nature, uplifting others and empowering women is reflected in her literary works.

Correspondence may be directed via email to:
lee.maywood.author@gmail.com

Acknowledgments

I would like to thank my family. My beautiful mother, Molly, a wonderful poet. Her lifelong sharing of poetry & dedication to literary appreciation sculpted my writing. My heartfelt gratitude to my late husband, Nate, his love & support has made so much possible, his laughter, quirkiness & humor filled life with color. I would like to voice my appreciation to my late father, Don, a fantastic artist, for teaching & encouraging me to sketch. My three sisters for their encouragement & help, Marita Luck for her literary ideas, corrections & advice over many years. Paula Flemons for her encouragement & inspiration. Jacinta Payne for her ideas, corrections, encouragement & nature inspirations. James Luck, an exceptional native bird & wildlife artist, wildlife advocate & an amazing brother, thank you for inspiring me to illustrate this book, because he 'only likes books that have pictures.' I would like to sincerely thank Geralyn Cheers for her encouragement from a young age & wonderfully creating my first poetry book many, many moons ago. My heartfelt appreciation to John Quinn (in loving memory) & John McCorquodale, their generosity & kindness helped the fruition of this project. I would like to extend my sincere gratitude to James Thayer, author of 13 critically acclaimed novels & a fantastic teacher of creative writing. Thank you for your help in evolving my literary skills. My appreciation & sincere thanks to IngramSpark for providing exceptional support & an extensive array of author services for publication, marketing, distribution & making the entire creation possible, thank you to Native Eden Publishing. Most importantly, my sincere thanks to my readers, loyally trudging the literary paths of my creations. I am so grateful, thank you for your support.

www.ingramcontent.com/pod-product-compliance
Lightning Source LLC
Chambersburg PA
CBHW020009140726
47904CB00018B/2137